BEK

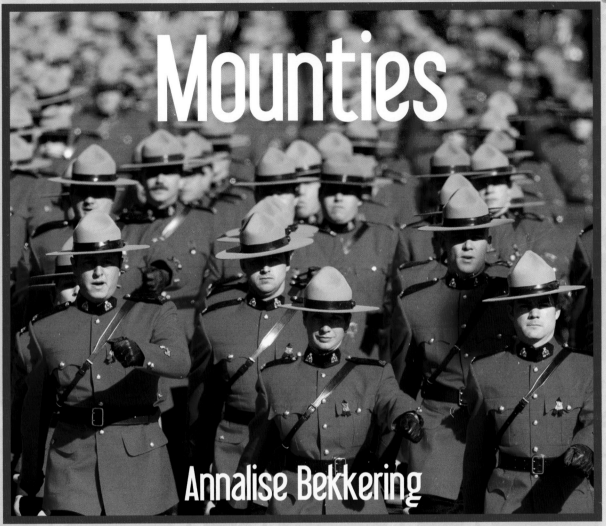

Mounties

Annalise Bekkering

Weigl

Published by Weigl Educational Publishers Limited
6325 10th Street SE
Calgary, Alberta T2H 2Z9
Website: www.weigl.com

Library and Archives Canada Cataloguing in Publication

Bekkering, Annalise
              Mounties : Canadian icons / Annalise Bekkering.
Includes index.
Also available in electronic format.
ISBN 978-1-77071-577-6 (bound).--ISBN 978-1-77071-584-4 (pbk.)
          1. Royal Canadian Mounted Police--Juvenile literature. I. Title.

HV8157.B44 2010   j363.2   C2010-903752-9

Printed in the United States of America in North Mankato, Minnesota
1 2 3 4 5 6 7 8 9 0 14 13 12 11 10

072010
WEP230610

Editor: Heather Kissock
Design: Terry Paulhus

Weigl acknowledges Getty Images, Alamy, Corbis, and Newscom as image suppliers for this title.

Every reasonable effort has been made to trace ownership and to obtain permission to reprint copyright material.
The publishers would be pleased to have any errors or omissions brought to their attention so that they may be
corrected in subsequent printings.

We acknowledge the financial support of the Government of Canada through the Canada Book Fund for our
publishing activities.

CONTENTS

What is a Mountie?

A Mountie is a member of the Royal Canadian Mounted Police (RCMP). The RCMP is Canada's national police force. Mounties are known throughout the world as a **symbol** of Canada.

Who were the First Mounties?

The RCMP began as the North-West Mounted Police (NWMP) in 1873. In 1920, the NWMP joined with Canada's other police force, the Dominion Police. Together, they became known as the Royal Canadian Mounted Police.

What is a Mountie's Job?

Mounties protect Canada and its people. There are more than 750 RCMP **detachments** across the country. Mounties patrol cities, towns, roads, and waterways. They also work in about 600 **Aboriginal** communities.

What Do Mounties Wear?

Mounties are known for the red uniform they wear to special events. This uniform is called the red serge. The RCMP also have uniforms for everyday use. These uniforms are made up of a grey shirt, dark blue tie, ankle boots, a cap, and dark blue pants with a gold stripe down each side.

The Red Serge

STETSON HAT A Stetson is a felt hat with a wide, flat brim. There is a dent in the top of the hat.

TUNIC The red jacket has a low collar and brass buttons.

BELT A Mountie's belt has a gun holster and pouches for handcuffs and bullets.

BREECHES Mounties wear black pants called breeches. Breeches have a yellow stripe down each leg. They bulge at the hips.

BOOTS Mounties wear brown leather riding boots. The boots have spurs.

11

Are Mounties Only in Canada?

Most Mounties work in Canada. Sometimes, they work in other countries. They have helped train police in countries such as Brazil, Russia, and Vietnam. Mounties also fought overseas for Canada in World War I and World War II. Today, they help in **peacekeeping missions** around the world.

Mountie Transportation

Mounties drive cars that have coloured lights, sirens, and computers. They also travel by bike, motorcycle, boat, and airplane. They use vans and trucks to carry equipment and police dogs. Some Mounties ride horses in parades and other events. In northern Canada, Mounties ride snowmobiles. They sometimes use dog sleds for special events.

What is the Musical Ride?

The Musical Ride is a group of 32 Mounties and horses that perform to music. During a show, they often do a move called the charge. The Mounties lower their lances, and the horses gallop across the field. The Musical Ride performs all over the world. It holds up to 50 shows each year.

Who Can Be a Mountie?

Only Canadian **citizens** can become Mounties. Canadians who want to join the RCMP must be at least 18 years old. They must have a driver's license, speak English or French, and have a high school diploma.

Where Do Mounties Train?

Mounties train at the RCMP Academy in Regina, Saskatchewan. Basic training lasts for 24 weeks. **Cadets** take classes in law and police work. They also learn how to drive a police car. After **graduation**, new Mounties spend six months training with experienced Mounties.

Make a Mountie Doll

Styrofoam ball

paper cup

brown paper

glue

plastic wiggle eyes

gold sequins

pink pen

red, black, brown, and pink craft foam

tape

pink, red, and black paint

1. Paint the ball pink, the bottom half of the cup red, and the top half black. Let dry, and then glue the ball to the bottom of the cup.

2. Cut two arms from red foam and two hands from pink foam. Glue one hand to the end of each arm and the other ends of the arms to the body. Cut two small rectangles of black foam, and glue one to each shoulder.

3. Cut a strip of brown paper, and glue it around the middle of the cup as a belt. Cut a thinner strip, and glue it around the body, bringing it up over one shoulder.

4. Use the brown paper to make a hat. Cut a circle for the brim. Then, cut a smaller circle out of the big circle so that it will sit on the ball. Cut a strip of brown foam, and tape it around the inside circle of the brim. Fasten the ends with glue. Cut a circle of brown foam. Tape it to the inside of the hat. Use glue to fasten the hat to the top of the Mountie's head.

5. Glue gold sequins onto the jacket to make buttons.

6. Add two eyes to the Mountie's head, and draw on a pink nose and mouth.

Find Out More

To learn more about Mounties, visit these websites.

Royal Canadian Mounted Police
www.rcmp-grc.gc.ca

The Fort Museum of the Northwest Mounted Police
www.nwmpmuseum.com

History of the RCMP
www.rcmphistory.ca

Musical Ride
www.rcmp-grc.gc.ca/fs-fd/
ride-equitation-eng.htm

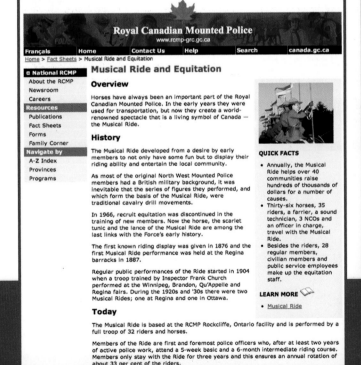

Glossary

Aboriginal: the original inhabitants of a country

cadets: students training to become soldiers or police officers

citizens: residents of a country who have the right to vote and other rights

detachments: branch offices of a police force

graduation: a ceremony marking the completion of a program

peacekeeping missions: the act of keeping peace in a foreign country

symbol: something that represents something else

Index

24